Prelude to Chaos

Prelude to Chaos

John V. Patrick

To order additional copies of this book, contact:
Xlibris Corporation
1-888-795-4274
www.Xlibris.com
Orders@Xlibris.com
62327

CONTENTS

Introduction

Chapters

Appendices

Dedications

This book is dedicated to my wife Dorothy whose advice, inspiration and patience made this book possible and to my daughter Lisa and son Marc for their confidence and encouragement.

INTRODUCTION

For at least the last ten years, we have attempted to improve our schools by proposing and executing change after change. We have spent an enormous amount of money on an inordinate number of new programs, and by any reasonable measure, our systems has gone backward.

Plummeting test scores, increased school dropout rates—some urban areas are reporting a dropout rate of over 40 percent, increases in teen pregnancies, increases in teen crime rate, and a student body that is disrespectful, conniving, selfish, hostile, and so disruptive that our teachers cannot effectively teach them and are part of our school problems.

The simple cause is that our children's needs are not being met, resulting in a form of neurosis with its own set of human traits and coping strategies. And as the children become adults, their needs remain unchanged, and the adults develop a new and different set of coping strategies—all based on the effects of deprived needs and a lack of self-actualization.

This book characterizes what we already know, have observed, and identified as real problems with our educational system; relates the identified problems to more in-depth causes; delves further into these causes; and proposes fundamentally different and unique solutions to the problems with our schools and our society.

The chapter units of this book are highly interrelated. Chapter 1 discusses the theory related to the neurosis caused by unfulfilled needs leading to disruptive students. Chapter 2 explains, in greater detail, how the developed neurosis affects our students, our schools and our society. The resulting accelerating degenerative effects on teachers and administrators; all resulting in our ineffective schools are explained in chapters 3 and 4. A unique solution to our dilemma is presented in chapter 5 while Chapter 7 presents ideas on how to execute the solution. And several factors which may help with the funding of our schools are discussed in Chapter 6.

CHAPTER 1

Psychology Theory

Our education systems and our schools are failing. For at least the last ten years, we have attempted to improve our schools by proposing and executing change after change. We have spent an enormous amount of money on an inordinate number of new programs, and by any reasonable measure, our schools have gone backward. At the present time, our government is poised to spend an additional humongous amount of money to redo (improve on) what we have been doing in the past fifty years—improving teacher efficiency, smaller schools and smaller class sizes, longer school days, better analysis of test data, and the list goes on.

Plummeting test scores, increased school dropout rates—some urban areas are reporting a dropout rate of over 40 percent, increases in teen pregnancies, increases in teen crime rate, and a student body that is disrespectful, conniving, selfish, angry, and so disruptive that our teachers cannot effectively teach them and are part of our school problems. The list goes on to include frustrated teachers and administrators culminating with our failing school system. These problems have now continued for several generations and are now affecting adults and many other aspects of our society.

We are also experiencing increased white-collar crime—especially fraud, a higher divorce rate, and may I add an increased number of dishonest politicians and civil strife.

The simple cause is that our children's needs are not being met, resulting in a form of neurosis with its own set of human traits and coping mechanisms. And as the children become adults, their needs remain unchanged, but the adults develop a new and different set of coping strategies—all based on the effects of deprived needs and a lack of self-actualization.

This book characterizes what we already know, have observed, and identified as real problems with our educational system; relates the identified problems to more in-depth causes, delves further into these causes, and proposes fundamentally different and unique solutions to the problems with our schools.

Our references to needs and neurosis are not treated in the classical sense. A college dictionary defined *neurosis* as a mild psychiatric disorder characterized by anxiety depression or hypochondria. We prefer a much-milder interpretation that relates neuroticism to inner needs and ego mainly directed toward others.

Several noted psychologist who pioneered work on self-actualization were Abraham Maslow (1908-1970), Kurt Goldstein, (1878-1965), and Karen Horney (1885-1952).

Maslow explicitly defines *self-actualization* to be the desire for self-fulfillment—mainly the tendency for the individual to become actualized in what he is potentially. This tendency might be rephrased as the desire to become more and more of what one is—to become everything that one is capable of becoming.

According to Kurt Goldstein, self-actualization is the tendency to actualize as much as possible the individual capacities. He felt the tendency to self-actualization is the only drive and abilities by which the life of an organism is determined and, therefore, determined the path of one's life.

A basic definition from a typical college textbook defines *self-actualization,* according to Maslow, simply as "the full realization of one's potential" without any mention of antiquated Goldstein. The most important difference between the two theories of self-actualization is the following:

For Goldstein, self-actualization was a motive; and for Maslow, it was a level of development. For both, however, roughly the same kinds of qualities were expressed: independence, autonomy, a tendency to form few but deep friendships, a philosophical sense of humor, a tendency to resist outside pressures, and a general transcendence of the human environment rather than a simple coping with it. Both expressed qualities related to fully actualized citizens (students).

Another favorite definition of self-actualization is man's attempt to be all that he thinks he can be, should be and want to be. *This definition connotes a strong relationship with self, society, one's ego and can be better linked to the theories of Karen Horney.*

Karen Horney developed one of the best known theories of neurosis. She believed that neurosis resulted from basic anxiety caused by interpersonal relationships. Her theory proposes that strategies used to cope with anxiety can be overused, causing them to take on the appearance of needs.

Scholars in the field of traditional psychoanalysis thinking will find Horney's theories quite different from most others. Most modern-day scholars are surprised by her now-familiar concepts on alienation, self-realization, the real self, the idealized self-image, and self-hate. She was considered a radical from the mainstream mostly because of her work on what was referred to as neurosis. Most traditionalists considered neurosis a psychotic defect. And her theories and work did not find favor with students of the motivational sciences. It is believed that had Horney used another description something other than neurotic needs to describe her theory; her works would have been more widely accepted among her colleges.

At that particular time, industrial as well as academic interest and money were mostly invested in the motivational aspects of physiology. In her book *Self-Analysis* (1942), Horney outlined the ten neurotic needs she had identified and the traits associated with the needs. These needs, when denied, altered or manipulated, form the bases for traits related to the demise of our school system and thus our society.

1. The Neurotic Need for Affection and Approval

These needs include the desires to be liked, to please other people, and to meet the expectations of others. People with this type of need are extremely sensitive to rejection and criticism and fear the anger or hostility of others.

2. The Neurotic Need for a Partner Who Will Take Over One's Life

These involve the need to be centered on a partner. People with this need suffer extreme fear of being abandoned by their partner. Oftentimes, these individuals place an exaggerated importance on love and believe that having a partner will resolve all of life's troubles. In the urban schools, especially at the middle school level, disruptions caused by friendships, jealousy, or lover's quarrel, and immature sex problems are common phenomena.

3. The Neurotic Need to Restrict One's Life within Narrow Borders

Individuals with this need prefer to remain inconspicuous and unnoticed. They are undemanding and content with little. They avoid wishing for material things, often making their own needs secondary and undervaluing their own talents and abilities. Shy and apparently timid students are common to this need.

4. The Neurotic Need for Power

Individuals with this need seek power for its own sake. They usually praise strength, despise weakness, and will exploit or dominate other people. These people fear personal limitations, helplessness, and uncontrollable situations.

5. The Neurotic Need to Exploit Others

These individuals view others in terms of what can be gained through association with them. People with this need generally pride themselves in their ability to exploit other people and are often focused on manipulating others to obtain desired objectives, including such things as ideas, power, money, or sex.

6. The Neurotic Need for Prestige

Individuals with a need for prestige value themselves in terms of public recognition and acclaim. Material possessions, personality characteristics, professional accomplishments, and loved ones are evaluated based on prestige value. These individuals often fear public embarrassment and loss of social status.

7. The Neurotic Need for Personal Admiration

Individuals with a neurotic need for personal admiration are narcissistic and have an exaggerated self-perception. They want to be admired based on this imagined self-view, not on how they really are.

8. The Neurotic Need for Personal Achievement

According to Horney, people push themselves to achieve greater and greater things as a result of basic insecurity. These individuals fear failure and feel a constant need to accomplish more than other people and to top even their own earlier successes.

9. The Neurotic Need for Self-sufficiency and Independence

These individuals exhibit a loner mentality, distancing themselves from others in order to avoid being tied down or dependent on other people.

10. The Neurotic Need for Perfection and Unassailability

These individuals constantly strive for complete infallibility. A common feature of this neurotic need is searching for personal flaws in order to quickly change or cover up these perceived imperfections.

It is obvious that the theories of Karen Horney can be correlated with traits exhibited by our students who are presently disrupting our schools, preventing teachers from doing their jobs of teaching them, and increasing the cost of their education.

> According to Horney, basic anxiety (and therefore neurosis) could result from a variety of things including, . . . direct or indirect domination, indifference, erratic behavior, lack of respect for the child's individual needs, lack of real guidance, disparaging attitudes, too much admiration or the absence of it, lack of reliable warmth, having to take sides in parental disagreements, too much or too little responsibility, over-protection, isolation from other children, injustice, discrimination, unkempt promises, hostile atmosphere, and so on and so on. (Horney, 1945)

Unfortunately, we often overlook the fact that in some schools, gang-type violence and bullying causes kids to forfeit their lunch money. If the students are hungry, their basic need (physiological) has not been met.

Consider the increased anxieties caused by the frustrations and pressures posed by our modern society and how they relate to the traits posed by the theories of Horney. The Horney theory of neurosis and the problems it outlines is easily extended beyond our high schools to our society at large. These neurotic effects tend to be more pronounced at the juvenile level where emotions run high. However, what should not be underestimated are the additional effects of multiple generations on this neurosis and the learned strategies passed between generations.

It is the tenor of this book that deprived self-actualization (unfulfilled needs) is the driving force of tensions that cause students to rebel and disrupt our schools. It is not enough that we depend on a system of parental or school discipline to control or modify the traits exhibited by our youth. *We must—through our system of education—replace, compensate for and modify these traits.* Modification by parental control is also hampered by a generation affect. The parents themselves can be infected by multiple generations of the neuroses and are not expected to execute effective corrections of the children.

A vivid example of the generation effect is the soccer dad who attacked the little league coach because he took his kid out of the game or attacks the referee because he feels the referee made a bad call. Some observers, depending on the generational effect of their own neuroses, would feel such incidences was caused by an enthusiastic or devoted parent's love for his child, while another observer without the neurotic tendencies would detest such actions.

The trend toward societal acceptance of the neurotic tendencies is a growing trend and presents a real and present danger to our school system. (*A Prelude to Chaos*)

CHAPTER 2

Trends in Student Behavior

Now that we have a broad overview of needs—how needs relate to motivation and personalities—and a glimpse at what some of the issues facing our school system and society are, let's take a look at modern observable trends in student behavior and take a look at the plethora of issues that plague our schools and the insights and recommendations that may resolve the problems.

Children's home environment shapes the initial constellation of attitudes they develop toward learning. When parents nurture their children's natural curiosity about the world by welcoming their questions, encouraging explorations, and familiarizing them with resources that can enlarge their world, they are giving their children the message that learning is worthwhile and frequently fun and satisfying. They are well on the road to becoming self-actualized.

When children are raised in a home that nurtures a sense of self-worth, competency, autonomy, and self-efficacy, they will be more apt to accept the risks inherent in learning. Conversely, when children do not view themselves as basically competent and able, their freedom to engage in academically challenging pursuits and capacity to tolerate and cope with failure are greatly diminished.

Once children start school, they begin forming beliefs about their school-related successes and failures. The sources to which children attribute their successes (commonly effort, ability, luck, or level of task difficulty) and failures (often lack of ability or lack of effort) have important implications for how they approach and cope with learning situations.

These children also form ideas of how their success relates to other people—the competitiveness and a meaning of success and all the related interactions that are related to success and failure. Once a student starts school, his interaction with more diverse people increases tremendously, and his needs that are related to the new interactions change, and so must his coping strategies change.

In many of our schools, violence and criminal activity is a problem. Any student who has to worry about his/her personal safety, whether he/she must "purchase" their safety through extortion, having his/her cell phone stolen, or having articles of clothing stolen from the gym locker will be motivated to ensure personal safety. Bullying and its related fear factors become strong influences in their lives. The need to become self actualized becomes more pronounced and demanding on his emotional wellbeing.

Especially in middle and high schools, students are searching for an identity. They are unsure of themselves, they feel awkward, and their bodies are changing. Emotionally, they long to separate from their parents. During tough economic times, many school systems try to trim their budgets by cutting back on extracurricular activities. In doing so, many students lose a significant portion of the only healthy social connection and avenues to self-actualization they have. Because of the generational effect poised a lack of self-actuation, we have tended to reduce the least competitive extracurricular activities in favor of the more competitive activities such as sports. Multiple generations of the neurotic effect tend to breed a love for competition.

Student behavior in intercity schools have become characterized by a growing defiant culture where students revel in such negative practices such as classroom disruptions, foul and vulgar language, teacher defiance, and almost any practice that they perceive as antiestablishment. There is a lack of respect for authority, and the students appear to enjoy being a part of this defiant culture. They magnify the old adage, "one bad apple ruins the whole barrel."

This book explores the causes of this explosion of behavior problems that lies at the root of intercity school failure—low test scores and increased dropout rates, increased criminal activity, increased sexual promiscuity and activity, increased teenage pregnancy, and excessive absences. These well-documented failures have generated several generations of books and research projects on how to improve student performance. Consultants have misdirected so much money and time toward these corrections that it cannot be counted.

Overall, most research into the areas of school improvement has served our education system well, and without them, our educational system would be worst. But problems in these areas continue to dramatically increase. Discipline problems in schools have increased exponentially.

The reason for the rapid growth of these trends in student behavior is that the students are using the defiant culture as a means of compensation for a lack of self-actualization. The consequence of deprived self-actualization is multifaceted and underestimated as to its effect on modern-day student behavior. Likewise, the methods by which humans strive for self-actualization can be easily correlated with the growing traits that are observed in urban schools. As theorized by Horney in chapter 1, an overuse of the struggle for self-actualization can lead to traits resembling neurosis and lead to increased and more diverse-coping strategies such as out-of-character personality tendencies which can lead further to major crime.

In the present-day schools, too many students are not accustomed to demanding and difficult class work. They prefer subjects as man and society or modern civilization. In such courses, students will often debate topics based on man's injustices to man and where they voice frustrations with humanity in open and often heated debate. These subjects, as taught in inter city schools, offer no real academic challenge to students. They are, more than less, a form of entertainment for the students. The debates are often encouraged by teachers under the disguise of student involvement, and they make classroom management easier.

These debates do offer a small opportunity for recognition and self-actualization, especially for the students who are more aggressive and talk the loudest.

A growing number of students rebel against teachers who teach in a traditional and demanding way—teachers who require students to think, search for, and discover answers to problems and situations. And a growing number of students are developing a dislike for the sciences and for mathematics where the demands for critical thinking are greater. They rebel against teachers who require that students generate data to substantiate what they think and use it in unique and creative ways to produce meaningful results. The target of consensus and other humanistic interactions are almost absent from these debates. Even in the more academically challenging classes, true academic performance is diminished as a source of self-actualization, and the classes become a source of frustration for far too many students.

Many books and even more articles have been written expounding the benefits of collaborative and group learning, interest approaches, and other techniques for teaching. Most have also served the teaching profession well. But again, none have solved the phenomenon of growing discipline problems and other classroom management problems presently experienced by teachers.

Modern teaching techniques and their positive effect on student behavior are well documented. But at this point, it is worth mentioning that the quest for self-actualization, especially in classroom situations, is notorious for classroom disruptions. The classroom disruptions are frequent because the needs are not readily or instantly met and can range from teacher disruptions such as talking out of turn to classroom fights. When deprived of neurotic needs (usually based on a lack of self-actualization), a strong or violent reaction can occur and does occur in far too many classrooms.

A dramatic example of a school disruption is the case of a disgruntled and frustrated student who walks out of class, lowers his pants, and defecates in the hallway in view of a monitoring camera. Another is the pregnant student who, in the middle of a laboratory class, raises her blouse and invites other students to feel her stomach as the baby moved. She appeared to be elated at the attention afforded by this. Both cases point to a neurotic need and a struggle for self-actualization. In these cases, defiance of school rules and a desire for recognition were the culprits and targets for self-actualization.

Additionally, student fights over whose method of solving a chemical problem have been observed even while the teacher gloated with elation at the apparent enthusiasm and desire for the student to be proven right at the demise of another student. Another is the game of chicken where two students walking toward each other in a game to see who would yield the space first have resulted in fights. The game of chicken is an obvious attempt at domination. There are numerous other cases of disruptions ranging from talking out of term to fights to deliberate put-downs (deliberately embarrassing another student). Some are minor class disruptions, and some are major crimes such as starting a fire in a wastebasket. A surprising number of these disrupting incidences can be directly correlated with Horney's description of neurotic needs gone wild.

Modern researchers have labeled poverty fueled by racial injustices as the generators of hopelessness and, thus, the perpetuators of trends toward decreased learning, increased student crime, increased teen pregnancy, and growing student negative attitudes toward authority—and learning and our system of educating students as the causes of our problems. And they are correct. Racial injustice and hopelessness are known to breed the most dramatic form of violent-coping strategies to a lack of self-actualization and, thus, neurosis.

The negative characteristics described here, especially as they are directed toward teachers and the school establishment, are fueled by a continuous drop in student learning and academic performance. Increased dropout rates and absences coupled with teen pregnancy are other indications of increased failures of our education system. The resulting pyramid of increased confusion and frustration for the students themselves and for the teachers who are charged with the inalienable task of directing the future of our kids and who must maintain the discipline and structure in the schools is the undisputed cause of our big problems.

These negative student characteristics that are extremely destructive in our urban schools have more than showed their colors in suburban schools and are presently weighing in at prestigious independent schools across the nation. A student arrested for massive graffiti was asked why he did it. His reply was that it made him feel good to ride through the town and see his tag displayed: an obvious attempt at self-actualization. But it was not clear whether his quest was born from his mental faculties.

Too many of our teachers, educators, administrators, and educational researchers have developed and do not hesitate to express all sorts of theories about why urban students are so mush more difficult to teach and why our test scores and academic performances continue to drop. Among these theories are the following:

- The bad teacher theory or the finger-pointing theory suggest that all teachers other than themselves are incompetent. The teachers themselves tend to fuel this theory.
- Low economic status of the students
- Generically defective students
- Sexually and physically abused students
- Neglected childhood
- Single heads of households
- English as a second language
- Large number of immigrants
- Economics of inner-city schools
- A lack of proper teacher training
- Lack of a uniform curriculum
- Underfunded schools

All of these theories are well documented as contributors to the observed student trends. However, their contributions individually or in any reasonable combination cannot be proven to contribute on a scale that would substantiate such large scale, rapidly developing, and uniform characteristics as we are presently experiencing in urban schools. Nor does any reasonable combination of theories carried out at reasonable levels really correlate. Thus, our directions of what we feel are needed is confusing and require drastic revision.

Unfortunately, researchers into the above factors as causes for school failure tend to research pockets of factors for study. In most cases, the interactions increase too rapidly and result in imperfect correlations.

Additionally, there are negative traits that do not appear to be related to the above theories. For example, plagiarism is common and dramatically growing. Most students know what it is, and that it is wrong, yet it continues to grow in intensity of violation and number of incidents. It is not enough for a student to copy the answer to an algebra problem or to copy homework. There are cases where students will turn in major projects where the only change is an inked-out and replaced name, or they will turn in last year's science project with the name replaced.

Consider apathy. The best correlation as to why it is increasing is indeed related to self-actualization. It is believed that apathy develops when the student has given up on obtaining self-actualization and has yielded to a form of withdrawal as listed by Horney (chapter 1). Be reminded that other factors or interactions may be involved, but the observable result is withdrawal.

The development of psychotic neurosis, whether temporally or permanently induced, is cited as a major cause of the observed student's behavior and is cited as a major cause of the big dilemma of failing schools.

Most of the efforts at improving our schools have been directed toward the areas expounded by educators and education researchers. These items are excellent targets for propaganda or excuses for our school failures. Teacher training in areas, expounding the psychological theories of Maslow, Goldstein, and Horney has been dramatically neglected; and for the average parent and high school graduate, these theories are nonexistent.

Critical thinking into areas of student behavior suggests that the causes are in the heads (mentally provoked) rather than physical in nature.

No reason can be found or has been presented as to why middle and high school curriculums cannot include psychological theory. It would certainly help all people understand one another and themselves. Such curriculum at the high school would also stimulate much more research into these areas. Such courses should be in-depth and mandatory in teacher preparation curriculums.

It is understood that psychological theory, especially at the high school level, can be controversial. But so are subjects such as sex education, patriotism, and moral ethics. Public sentiment against teaching these subjects as part of high school curriculum appears to be lessening. Educators and education researchers can do much more toward influencing public attitude and toward the need for such curriculum.

More on the subject of teaching psychological theory will be presented in chapter 7.

CHAPTER 3

Present-Day Teachers

For the most part, teachers are the unsung heroes of most school systems. Yet they are considered, by popular belief, to be the purveyors of most of the problems in schools. Administrators and teacher educators express the need for more and better teacher training, elimination of teacher unions, reduced class size, better pedagogy, the need for a more uniform curriculum, problems with special education, better classroom management, better school atmosphere—and the list goes on and includes a need for better school management. But when teachers and their problems are looked at with a critical scientific eye, a different view of their performance rating is seen, and their problems and needs emerge and so do several new theories.

These theories suggest that teachers are the victims rather than the culprits. To their dismay, teachers have fallen prey to the characteristics exhibited by the children and the inability of society and our education system to make the necessary and appropriate adjustments. Teacher unions, trade organization, and administrators have been of little or no help to the teachers because the prevailing theories and, thus, most of their efforts at helping the teachers have been based on those causes outlined in chapter 2. Teachers are their own best critics. Their conversations only need a keen ear and analysis of their complaints.

The following are excerpts of the present-day teachers' conversations about teaching:

1. Sometimes I fear that we will lose faith—faith in ourselves and our children. Many teachers find their classes harder, their children

demonstrating fewer academic and social skills. In my school too, the challenges can be daunting. More than ever, we need to feel the courage and hope of our professions. We need the time and stamina to problem-solve, to search in our own midst for effective strategies, and to collaborate.

2. Classes had been dismissed for lunch, and the hallway was alive with kids going into lockers, heading for restrooms, and meeting friends . . . I saw Patricia and James playfully arguing. Suddenly, with the grace of a dancer, Patricia's leg shot out and kicked a laughing James with a sideswipe worthy of Jean-Claude Van Damme.

3. My biggest stress has to do with the issues that kids come to school with that are so difficult to identify. I've had these children for two months almost [this school year], and there are still issues that hold up their educational process. I talk to parents but still can't get the children to attend to the task given. It's not an academic problem; it's a social problem.
   Getting kids to open up, developing the skills needed to create independent problem-solvers, developing respect among students, and getting kids to take responsibility for their own learning—these are the sorts of problems teachers face every day—big problems without simple answers.

4. With the lessons right now, my biggest issue is behavior management, getting control of the class to get across effectively. When you have a class size that is pretty much at a capacity of thirty-two kids, the room is filled, and you never have everyone on task and focused.

5. It seems that over the years my students have become increasingly nonverbal and passive . . . They need to be prodded to express themselves in a class discussion or to share something about themselves. When they do speak, they offer only the required amount of information.

6. Differentiating instructions so that the needs and learning styles of all students are met is a constant source of stress. The No Child Left Behind motto is one that teachers take very seriously, but constantly struggle with how to accomplish the goal.

7. This is my sixteenth year teaching secondary English, and what seems to be wearing me down is the paper load. The multiple choice and short-answer questions are relatively manageable, but the essays and research projects are a burden. They consume three to four hours of each Saturday morning, and as happy as I am to wake up to a day without bells, the stack of essays [to grade] sits like a weight on my spirits. Occasionally, I conduct peer-editing and self-editing lessons, but still have not found a way to significantly reduce the long hours.

8. For the modern educator, there is no greater stress than wanting to succeed admirably at an important task and being systematically denied the resources to do so, but that is precisely the fate awaiting most who undertake the job of teaching. To paraphrase the old real estate adage, the three secrets of effective teaching are time, time, and time. The requirements for presenting excellent instruction are time to plan effective lessons, time to present those lessons, and, finally, time to assess whether learning has taken place. All three are absolutely essential to improving student achievement.

9. Today, however, good teaching transpires mostly where teachers donate innumerable hours of uncompensated time to the schools for the purposes of planning and assessment Teachers in your typical school are in front of children for 275 minutes a day, and if they are fortunate, they have a paltry forty-five minutes to plan their lessons. The remainder of a teacher's requisite planning must be performed outside the seven hours.

10. My biggest professional stress is trying to motivate students to learn when they don't have any motivation coming in. A lot of kids have not hooked into the fact that learning is important to them.

11. Because it's boring, I am a junior. We get tired of boring teachers. Like me, I am in chemistry; my teacher, he is awesome! He makes us laugh. And he makes jokes about the work we do. I mean, he makes things interesting. He is also crazy in a way. And all we get graded for are their test and lab reports. It's hard, but he has motivated us to pass his class because he has made it to where he will be the next physics teacher next year.

The above excerpts characterize our present-day teachers who love teaching, who love their jobs, but are losing the battle. The frustrations caused by neurotic, disgruntled students with unfilled needs, coupled with the loud voices of disgruntled parents and pushy administrators are daunting. Disgruntled parents usually turn to administrators for help when problems arise. The administrators often do not analyze these problems but will approach the teacher, often with disdain, leading to a more frustrated teacher.

Once the frustrations of trying to teach sets in, most teachers, especially teachers of urban students, appear to be resolved that the teaching of the defiant students is impossible; and they do not hesitate to voice their theories. But the problem of greater consequence, regardless of its origin is the teacher who believes that the students cannot learn. A teacher who does not believe the students can learn is useless. For example, some teachers might believe a student cannot learn algebra or chemistry because the subject matter is too difficult.

When asked about the cause of our failing schools, teachers echo the classical theories outlined in chapter 2 as the main culprits causing our dilemma. One characteristic of teachers do not readily expressed but on close observation becomes obvious is that of an underlying fear of the students. Most teachers have a fear of physical harm from students because most teachers are females, and especially in high schools, physical harm from an angry student is a logical reaction. In urban schools, the fear factor is much greater to the extent that recruiting the better teachers becomes a problem.

Another fear of teachers is that of political reprisal. It is not unusual for students to report what they may consider an infraction of the rules by a teacher to an administrator. Such reports and accusations, whether true or false, are a source of great frustration to a teacher.

These theories and the teachers themselves are easy targets of prey for the more vocal critics of our schools as well as educational researchers, mostly because they have none better to blame. The lack of classroom management skills is the favorite target used by first-echelon administrators who are usually responsible for discipline matters. Teachers who do not present them with discipline problems are their favorites and will receive their loud and clear praises.

The teachers, especially the more experienced ones, become resolved that the best way to handle defiant student behavior and prevent problems with administrators is through appeasement of the students. They have become very astute at alleviating rowdy and defiant student's problems using day-to-day remedies. Their remedies are time-consuming at the expense of real academics, and these offer little or no effectiveness toward improving student performance. Because their jobs are so daunting, the main goal of most urban teachers begins to focus on getting through the day.

Adding to the problem, students will observe, analyze, and learn the habits of teachers with the skill of a seasoned research scientist and go into action with their own remedies, often at the expense of the teacher. They are very astute at breaking the spirit of a teacher who actually tries to teach. Too many students have bragged about how they break the spirit of teachers and will make wagers on how long a new teacher will last.

There are far too many teachers who really like the job teaching. But because of the defiant, rowdy, and unmotivated students, they are finding their job frustrating, if not impossible. Administrators tend to join with the pacifying teachers and do not require that they teach. They require only that the teachers keep order and reduce discipline problems.

> Students will observe, analyze, and learn the habits of teachers with the skill of a seasoned research scientist and go into action with their own remedies, often at the expense of the teacher then, brag about it.

Teachers will mollify the students with trivia work that the student can successfully do with little or no effort. This seems to pacify the students, and they are happy with the apparent self-actualization that the easy work affords. Students are quick to tell a trying teacher, "You cannot teach, or you are the only teacher I have trouble with."

Another approach at pacifying the students is simply to entertain them. Chemistry classes are always boring unless something burns or explores. Present-day pedagogy dictates an interest approach at the start of each class. This sounds good and has served the teachers well, mostly because the student's voice expressing boredom and frustration with teachers is loud and clear. The interest approach that does not last for the whole class period is useless toward effective teaching. Students tend to cling to the interesting approach and resent the nitty-gritty of the related real class.

In far too many classes, student lose interest when the topic is changed or even the emphasis is changed to a different point of view. Some teachers feel this drop in interest is due to attention deficit disorders, but there is ample evidence that it is a type of rejection message to the teacher.

Quiet students are often allowed to sit in the rear of the class and doodle as long as they do not disturb the class. Students learn quickly that this and a smile will please the teacher, and they will pass the class.

The problems of teachers are directly related to failing schools. Maybe we should call these "the practices of teachers" rather than "the problems of teacher." They raise the question, "What comes first, the chicken or the egg?" Negative practices by teachers certainly do not improve the situations of poor student performance, but it is not the true cause of our failing schools. The need for and the struggle for students to obtain self-actualization appears to be the reason for defiant students, classroom management problems, low test scores, teacher frustration, high turnover rates of teachers, high dropout rates of students, and a whole host of problems related to our dilemma of poor-performing schools.

The schools that have lower *dropout rates* and better behaved students provide quality teaching that is relevant. True or false?

The following is indicative of the prevailing pedagogy advocated in present-day teacher education schools. It is obviously correct and true but is a long way from what is necessary to solve the present dilemma of defiant children in our schools. The need to change the mind-set of today's youth has never been more obvious.

The following is from copyright © 2004, the Parent Institute®, a division of NIS, Inc., www.parent-institute.com. Reproduction rights exclusively for South Brunswick Public Schools, EPIC Program.

1. Discipline means "to teach"—it does not mean "to punish." Accordingly, it should be done out of love.
2. Consistency is key. No matter what approach you take to discipline, it's crucial to be consistent about it. In other words, this morning's rules should also apply this afternoon.
3. Be patient. No discipline strategy works all the time—but that doesn't mean the strategy isn't working overall.
4. Children need and want limits. Effective discipline doesn't stifle kids—it gives them a strong, dependable foundation from which to grow and mature.

5. Discipline isn't just about correcting what your child does wrong—it's about celebrating what he does right. The more you praise and reinforce the good things he does, the better.

Discipline Issues and Boredom

Teaching is a very tough profession. Teachers are expected to juggle so many issues each day that the most patient person would soon suffer from fatigue. But a new British study reveals that when students are frustrated with repeated substitute teachers, poor teaching methods, and poor leadership, they misbehave.

Administrators were busy working on school reform, and teachers lacked leadership. However, the study found that teachers who developed relationships with students and varied how they taught classes had few discipline problems. (Barbara Pytel, 2006)

Most schools have extensive and expensive professional development programs for teachers. These programs are usually so extensive and expensive that any reasonable person has to ask the question, "If such extensive retraining of teachers is necessary, why do we require teacher certification and standard qualifications for teachers?" Why can't the certified teacher just walk into the classroom ready to teach? This would certainly help with cost.

After returning to teaching from a thirty-five year hiatus and observing teaching and learning, an old-timer was asked for an opinion of what went wrong to cause such a dramatic change in schools. After a long hesitation, she replied, "Things changed when we started listening to the kids." Continuing the conversation revealed that her reference to "the kids" meant that she felt kids were running the schools—determining policy, curriculum, activities, and schedules and basically running the schools. It is believed that her comments are basically true, and the described situation is born from attempts to pacify student and parents.

Part of the problem with teacher—student relations is that the school systems have excessively acquiesced to the students. A bored student is a legitimate excuse for the student and it is the teachers fault.

Teaching is a formidable task, and the extensive need for such expensive professional development programs for teachers is indicative of how serious the failing school situation has become. And professional development for teachers is an expensive mandate in far too many schools, often at the expense of class size and other programs related to cost.

The diversity of personal issues, motives derived from neurotic needs of students, the copycat issue (the one rotten apple) coupled with problems posed by students with legitimate learning disabilities—all present in one classroom on any given day—are so complex that no teacher can be expected to negotiate an effective class.

The issue of special education adds a phenomenal dimension of diversity to the school system. And because of the broad range of diverse issues it brings to the classroom, it presents an even broader range of problems for the system and even more for the individual teacher (annex 6). Further, and no doubt because of cost constraints, a system called "inclusion" was devised and added to the teacher's burden.

The Individuals with Disabilities Education Act (IDEA) is the public school's special education legal basis of how and what programs will be in place for the special-needs student. IDEA mandates that special education students be placed in the least restrictive environment with the appropriate supports. The most common interpretation of this law is "Wherever possible, special-needs students should be placed in the regular classrooms." Such students may include students with attention deficit and behavior disorders coupled with an assortment of learning disorders.

It is theorized that 13.5 percent of students qualify for special education and another 13.5 percent are undiagnosed. This data added to the undetermined number of students whose neurotic needs are not being met adds to the problems with teaching and discipline and our failing schools. It is extremely difficult to explain how school officials expect a teacher to negotiate effective teaching in the typical urban high school classroom.

"Inclusive education means teachers working with students in a context that is suitable to a diverse population of students. It also means the teacher may need alternative expectations and goals for students, and it's difficult to get teachers to do this" (Dr. Kathy East, support services coordinator, Price Laboratory School, UNI).

Educating teachers on the neurotic needs of students would without a doubt help the situation, but is not within itself a total solution or guarantee to solve all the discipline problems. The teaching of psychology and the neurotic needs of students is not presently a major item within the curriculum for teacher education, at least not in the form that it should be. More on this subject is presented in chapter 4.

The mandates placed on our school officials are tremendous. But the effective performances required to negotiate the requirements placed on them are considered poor. The recommendation to teach self-actualization and to eliminate the problems set forth in this book to improve the characteristics of teachers, students, and administrations is but a tip of what is needed to establish an effective school system. Problems exist in almost all areas of educational management.

CHAPTER 4

The Administration

The academic failure of schools can be strongly linked to student behavior. School administrator superintendents, principals, and teachers have been identified as the first echelon of cadre directly responsible for regulating student behavior. Problems with student behavior are well documented as rapidly increasing to catastrophic levels, especially in the urban schools, and are rapidly spreading to the suburban and private schools. Logic suggests that regulation of the student behavior must be elevated beyond the classic first-echelon administrative responsibilities to teacher colleges, state, and perhaps, the federal level. There is no doubt that more effective involvement is required.

Classic theory and research suggest that family income and other social factors have significant influence on academic performance of students. It is also believed that these are valid factors and a strong influence on the disruptive behavior exhibited by students. But it is also believed that the student behavior is directly and strongly related to a lack of self-actualization, which is the most significant culprit causing the disruptive behavior. It is also believed that administrators at all echelons and those responsible for teacher education and curriculum have been remiss in developing effective strategies to combat this growing trend. We must take decisive action to combat the trend.

Just as important, we believed that the self-actualization theories go beyond student behavior to all human behavior and involve such social factors as crime, divorce rates, domestic violence, and other areas where social interaction between people is the driving forces. In other words, we must change human behavior.

To change human behavior sounds like a large if not impossible task. But consider that when we teach a new concept to a student or influence how someone thinks about or acts on anything, we are indeed changing their behavior. Therefore, if we start at the lower grades and teach the meaning and effect of self-actualization and the effect of being denied self-actualization, we will have made a tremendous contribution to humanity and how students think about and view one another and themselves. This knowledge will also help with crime rates, domestic problems, and with almost any problems dealing with human interactions. The students will grow up more self-actualized—a better knowledge of how they feel about themselves and their fellow man—and so will their children and their children's children.

The goal of teaching self-actualization becomes more realistic when we consider in the 1950s, patriotism was taught to high school students through civics classes among other avenues and was quite effective in teaching pride in one's country as well as pride in one's self. Respect from others and the pride that one will gain when it is recognized how respect by others is gained and is not an entitlement will be a tremendous benefactor.

At present, our students appear to feel that respect from others is obtained through intimidation, finagling, lying, and cheating and through other psychological manipulations. We can change our culture through educating our students about self-actualization and the related philosophy of personalities.

Recently, there are tendencies for the federal and state governments to do the heavy lifting with respect to curriculum development, or as some would say curriculum improvement. Effort is presently under way to move toward a unified and standardized curriculum for all schools and all subjects. Such a move is costly and does not work because a uniform curriculum and teachings tends to stifle ingenuity.

There are several other rationales for this movement that suggest it would benefit students who move from school to school by making all teaching and learning the same. Besides being costly, uniform curriculums, even when done properly, tend to be developed from the top down and do not provide for the needs of the local community or for the needs of local teachers. For example, some communities may be more industrially oriented as opposed to academically oriented. Or the chemistry teacher may have been trained in biochemistry rather than physical chemistry. While the results of their teaching would hopefully be the same; their approach to a particular unit may be different. This could cause problems with testing, especially with benchmarks and other test, especially mandated testing.

More importantly, most teachers will tell you that it is easier and more efficient when they teach lessons they develop rather than lessons developed by someone else. This does not mean that colleges, universities, and administrators cannot guide and make suggestions about curriculum. Teachers should develop their lessons to predetermined standards.

It is easier and more efficient for teachers to adjust their lessons to existing standards as it does not require a great infusion of time and money. Dialogue between teachers and across disciplines is extremely important. It has been observed that a topic as simple as conversion factors was taught in all science courses from six through twelfth grades and again in some math courses. The same can be said for scientific notation. Likewise, an administrative review of the adjusted lessons by upper-echelon administration is important.

It is strongly advocated that curriculum development of standards should be better coordinated with the colleges, universities and to the local school districts with strong input from the teachers. The federal government is best at establishing policy. Who would know more about teaching chemistry than a chemist? On the other hand, who would know more about pedagogy than a teacher? These suggest that teacher colleges and universities must assume more of the heavy lifting with better input from state and federal government. The teacher colleges, through better coordination and influence as educators of teachers, should exert more influence on what actually happens in the classroom. Yet they should not be so over controlling that creativity is stifled.

Coordination of curriculum is much more important than who teaches it. With the present state of things, a teacher may be confronted with a mandate to teach a subject from the federal government, which is interpreted by the state educators, rewritten by the local district, and supervised by the principal and by the various department heads.

Because of economical constraints, we have changed or eliminated too many courses by which students gained in self-actualization. In far too many schools, art, music, dance, drama, sports, and other subjects that tend to be socially oriented have been reduced or eliminated. These subjects have traditionally provided a source for self-actualization and individual pride for students.

There are sound arguments against most presently advocated remedies such as merit pay for teachers, charter schools, smaller schools, and better teacher education. Merit pay has been tried enough for us to know if it really works. Apparently, it has caused dissention among teachers because there was no equitable evaluation system in place. Teacher evaluation systems tend to cause teacher-to-teacher conflicts and accusations of favoritism.

Charter schools connote selective education either through the application process or through political manipulations. The concept of themed schools (themed charter schools) suggest location and racial patterns are factors and, thus, selective education. If not, politicians will most likely make these issues. There are areas in close proximity to large urban schools where the private schools are over run with applications. Mostly because of the problems of poor performance, discipline and high crime exhibited by the public schools.

Increased education for teachers cannot be correlated with the humongous amount of money already being spent on professional development for teachers.

Of the above remedies, selective education appears more practical for solving the current discipline problems; at least for now and the apparent success of our elite private schools will attest to it. But is a system based totally on elite private schools economically and socially practical for all students? Are discipline problems at elite private schools increasing? We should look carefully at the selective success of charter schools, or we will rediscover the wheel. Our society is so hungry for effective schools that are not plagued with the discipline problems and poor academic performance; they tend to grab for what appears to be a solution. There are too many interacting variables to pinpoint the reason affecting the erratic successes of charter schools.

Since cost constraints appear to be a driving force that has led to changes affecting actualization of students such as the elimination of socially oriented programs, administrators must be more creative with methods that could save cost. For example, there are subjects that could be taught within large classes, thereby reducing the number of certified teachers required.

The military has a cost-effective system and has been quite successful with mass instructions, especially when the students are later reduced to smaller groups for practical exercises. Most schools could save a tremendous amount of money using this technique. It should work even with some type of math courses and with self-actualization classes. When this concept is discussed with teachers and first-echelon administrators, their rationale for not using it is because of discipline problems that develop in large classes. This again underscores the problems and cost posed by discipline problems.

Present-day educators and administrators have concentrated on teacher education, classroom management and have emphasized the same tired arguments such as course sequence, pedagogy, who should take certain courses, and who should attend certain schools. No child left behind has consumed an inordinate amount of our educators' and administrators' time and our money.

The following are two excerpts from the Brookings Institute at Brown University. It underscores some of the recent concerns over educational policy.

The push for universal eighth-grade algebra is based on an argument for equity, not on empirical evidence. General or remedial math courses tend to be curricular dead-ends, leading to more courses with the same title (for example, General Math 9, General Math 10) and no real progression in mathematical content. By completing algebra in eighth grade—and then completing a sequence of geometry as freshmen, advanced algebra as sophomores, and trigonometry, math analysis, or pre-calculus as juniors—students are able to take calculus in the senior year of high school. Waiting until ninth grade to take algebra makes taking calculus in high school more difficult. From this point of view, expanding eighth-grade algebra to include all students opens up opportunities for advancement to students who previously had not been afforded them, in particular, students of color and from poor families. Democratizing eighth-grade algebra promotes social justice.

Incentives shape behavior. Some analysts today express the concern that, by focusing attention on the education of students at the bottom of the achievement distribution, NCLB is surely encouraging schools to neglect high achievers. After all, schools face consequences for failing to move low achieving students to proficiency. Students in schools that fail to make adequate progress for two consecutive years must be offered the option of transferring to another public school. A school that continues to fall short faces possible replacement of its teaching staff. Conversion to a charter school, or with a state takeover. Nothing, however, happens when schools fail to boost the learning of already-proficient students to higher levels. As Susan Goodkin argued in the Washington Post, "By forcing schools to focus their time and funding almost entirely on bringing Low achieving students up to proficiency, NCLB sacrifices the education of the gifted students who will become our future biomedical researchers, computer engineers, and other scientific leaders.

Another major policy change has involved the sequence of teaching physics, chemistry, and general science and resulted in the teaching of a watered-down physics course first. This sequence and course selection was touted as better science for the twentieth century and also resulted with certification requirements for physics teachers. The overall program bordered on deception and again suggests that neurosis is on the move upward.

It should be obvious that we cannot continue to believe that we can control student behavior with a strong system of student discipline and course manipulations along.

Considering that our schools are at crisis stage of ineffectiveness, it is suggested that we should not be having these arguments as presented above and most defiantly should have spent our money and energy more wisely.

In the present-day schools, first-echelon administrators spend an inordinate amount of time with discipline problems, parent concerns mostly related to discipline, teacher management, and other operational concerns such as bus, cafeteria, and sports management, grades, and to a lesser extent, curriculum matters. Looking beyond the first-echelon school management, we find layers and layers of redundant management. The following might shed some light on redundant management concerns involving discipline.

Most administrators will suggest that discipline problems start in the classroom. Some teachers will agree that a great number of discipline problems start in the classroom but disagree as to why.

Teachers are responsible for discipline in the classroom, but have no recourse but to call for help when a problem arises and must often wait to put out the fire. The teacher must explain in detail to the administrator and document what has happened. The administrator must redocument what has happened and document how the incident was resolved (detention, suspension, parent involvement, etc.).

Teachers usually can give a maximum of fifteen minutes of detention. However, most students do not report on time for detention. They report late with excuses such as had to use the restroom, had to call their parents, forgot they had detention, had to talk to another teacher, or had detention from another teacher. This leaves the teacher with an accounting problem, another documentation problem, and a longer nonacademic day. Then there is the in-school detention, usually controlled by the principal and which provides the students with another excuse as to why they did not report to their teacher's detention. Given the educational requirements placed on teachers, it would suggest that teachers could be more directly responsible for punishing some types of student infractions similar to that used by the military article 15 offenses. Such a system must be studied in detail before implemented. But once in place, it would help reduce discipline problems and the amount of time spent by all administrators on discipline issues.

The military's article 15 policy authorizes commanding officers the authority to punish minor infractions in lieu of a court-martial. It is usually swift, expedient, and it covers the most frequently committed offenses.

Most school districts require that teachers be certified with at least a bachelor's degree and have extensive professional development programs to boost the effectiveness of already certified teachers. Yet administrators spend an inordinate amount of money and time with teacher's supervision. Often, there are department heads, lead teachers, and administrators for each of the main disciplines. Such organizational structure does not seem necessary and often leads to over managed and frustrated teachers. If the teacher colleges began lifting their loads properly, we can reduce cost by reducing redundant management. Because of the cationic condition of our schools, the apparent need for multiple layers of management has grown. As noted by Horney (chapter 1), we tend to seek saviors rather than practical or logical solutions to our problems, and thus, we produce layers and layers of redundant management.

The functional organization of most schools start with the superintendent who is strongly influenced by the political objectives of the board of directors. The superintendent establishes line and dotted line organizational positions according to perceived needs, which are usually temporary in nature. Regardless of the derived organization or how often it changes, the administrators and their staff spend an inordinate amount of time on parent appeasements related to the political orientation and discipline related to the parents of individual students (see appendix "A Day in the Life of an Administrator"). The organizational structure also results in organizational hierarchy with emphasis on the same tired areas and issues as listed in chapter 2.

Many researchers have suggested that board turnover is a major reason that relationships deteriorate. New members on a board may not support the initiatives under way or the personal qualities that previous board members felt were important. The turnover of board members is often cited as a main reason that school initiatives are abandoned, and mistrust develops. This situation is especially difficult when a new member has a mandate from constituents that he or she pursues with significant energy.

Board members are increasingly paying attention to their political constituents and getting reelected. Very active political board members' decisions are viewed in the opinion of many superintendents as more with an eye to what will gain the support of voters rather than what is best for the children. Tough decisions that alienate voters can result in loss of support from the board, even if the decisions are best for the school system over the long haul. Educational leaders have learned that they must have board support if they or their initiatives are to whether the heat that accompanies almost every decision.

An example of this phenomenon occurred in a very hotly debated vote to approve condom distribution in Philadelphia and New York. Philadelphia superintendent, Constance Clayton, was able to get the school board to propose and support the idea. New York Chancellor Joseph Fernandez was eventually unseated by his political battles with the board and community over issues such as condom distribution; the chancellor was called King Condom by a number of board and community members. Superintendents necessarily face controversial issues, and they will be in trouble if their boards do not stick with them and provide support.

It appears as if the political game actually starts at the top with the school boards. However, some school boards actually are appointed by the mayor. When the school policies start with a state-appointed commissioner of education, the educational policies are just as much controlled by politics.

In most school systems, teachers are hired by the superintendent. A new trend introduced the concept of site-based managed schools. With this concept, each school stands as a more independent unit. Site-based managed schools are public schools where the authority and responsibility to run the school have been passed down from the district office to a school management team. The team includes the principal, other school-level staff, and local community delegates—usually parents of children in the school. Usually a committee within the team hires the teachers.

Site-based management depends on collaboration and teamwork among teachers, administrators, and parents. Collaborative decision making in educational systems is frequently characterized by conflict and disagreement, given differing perspectives and opinions among participants, and different interest groups. Beside, the expected conflict between parents with special interest in their own kids, union rules take center stage. When site-based schools are forming, usually there is conflict with the local union, mostly centered on work rules with the hiring of teachers as the main issues.

One of the main issues considered when the hiring committees select a teacher is that of compatibility within the school. This suggests that the resulting teachers will look alike, think alike, and smell alike. The number of minority teachers, and in some cases, the number of male teachers will continue to diminish.

It is believed that teacher preparation by the teacher colleges and universities should be the main focus for improving teacher efficiency. Coordination between teachers and curriculum planning should be the main focus of the presently so-called and costly professional development programs. The hiring of teachers should be based on criterion similar to that used by industry—academic preparation, previous work history (experience), recommendations, and interview and needs.

It is also believed that a main objective of site-based management concept is to break the control of teacher unions. Most school boards, superintendents, and school systems feel that balancing their budgets is dependent on the demise of teacher unions, which control teacher salaries, class size, and whole host of work rules including hiring and firing of teachers. The present state of the political climate suggests that teachers are the main culprits causing failing schools, and it is beyond an indication that teacher unions are the main targets of this belief.

Like charter schools, the overall judgment of site-based schools is still out to lunch. Both are new concepts, and there is considerable doubt that either will get a fair and impartial evaluation, mostly because of vested interest. Every public official or politician who has ever recommended or advocated an issue concerning schools has a vested interest in these concepts and the glory that their advocacy will bring. Other concerns with heavy political interest include graduation rates and test scores from these type schools (annex 9).

Traditionally, urban high schools have been large with an enrollment around 1,800 students each. Some districts have broken these schools into smaller units based on all sorts of rationale centered on a more personalization of the student environment. For example, one school with 1,800 students was broken into three site-based units of about six hundred each with three different academic themes. The benefits of this decentralization are not known. But the obvious negative results were the following:

1. A drop in esprit de corps based on sports and other factors related to self-actualization of students. For example, it would be more difficult to arrange a dance cotillion involving one smaller academic unit.
2. Problems with scheduling and course offerings within and between the different academic units. Often this type problem results in the

intermingling of students within a single class, and this brings us back to the original large school concept.

3. A reduction in teacher collaboration between units.

4. An increase in administrative cost—more redundancy. This factor leads one to question why larger high schools were conceived and developed in the first place. Large school are more cost efficient.

CHAPTER 5

Behavior: The Ultimate Objective

Chapters 4 suggests that the needs of our students and their quest for self-actualization have yielded students that are dominating, manipulating, and selfish, dishonest, greedy, intimidating, and a host of other traits showing neurotic tendencies. This has led to massive disruption in our schools. One has to wonder when and how this got started. The trend appears to have developed gradually but is now accelerating at an exponential rate and is engulfing other factions of our society.

Looking at the publicized mentality of our present-day business and political world shows that greed also fits the trend. When one looks at the need for success in the business world, there is a direct correlation with the need for self-actualization and traits exhibited by our students. I will hesitate before I say that the adult world suffers from the exact neurosis as our kids, but it is believed that when the needs of the business leaders and politicians are not met, neurosis can develop.

In the popular movie *Wall Street*, Michael Douglas coined the phrase "Greed is good," suggesting that everything is fair that gets results. Maybe this was the beginning of a mentality that has engulfed our society. One only need to look at the number of high-tech crimes based on greed, manipulations, fraud, domination, lies, and other disruptive characteristics. There is a direct correlation with what we are experiencing in our schools. The major difference is that, in our schools, the actions by students seeking self-actualization are less sophisticated. Consider the following:

1. Leading presidential candidate appoints virtually unknown as his running mate for VP.

2. Finance leaders pay out lucrative bonuses after receiving governmental payout funds.
3. Governor denies trying to sell senate seat after government produces tapes as evidence.
4. Auto leaders report to congressional hearing on bailout request in private jets.
5. President goes to war over weapons of mass destruction after being advised that the weapons do not exist.
6. Married president has sex affair and confesses to the nation that he did it because he could.
7. Presidential candidate reported that she was dodging sniper fire when in fact she was not.
8. Weapons supplied to Mexican drug cartel by American business runs wild.
9. Sniper on rampage.
10. Official goes to jail for 25-billion dollar Ponzi scheme.

One could rationalize these reported incidents as trivia caused by inaccurate reporting by the press, minor mistakes in judgment, are psychotically derived, or any number of other excuses or factors. But in each of the above, the reported propitiator would be expected to exhibit the highest level of conduct, integrity, or business consistent with good rationale and moral law. Each involves a thought process that resulted in an action. It is believed that a form of neurosis, hopefully a temporary form, caused these incidents. All correlates well with neurosis according to the theories of Horney. Greed at the expense of others is a form of neurosis.

Maybe the famous phrase by Michael Douglas was the beginning. One only needs to listen to television or read the press to experience the proliferation of predator crimes and incidence of fraud. Are our students mimicking adults, or is it that our neurotic students have grown up and we are beginning to accept the neurotic behavior?

Disruptive behavior in our schools is worst in the middle schools where students are less mature and their mental processes are more susceptible to manipulation by unfulfilled needs. The reactions when needs of middle school students are not met are more intense, more spontaneous, and therefore, more disruptive to the teachers. Likewise, the neurosis-related needs in urban areas are more intense and more abundant. The urban student has also experienced a greater variety of deprivations.

Imagine that you commute to work. Your car is in a state of disrepair. The tires are bald, the brakes screech; you need wiper blades, and you have plastic over a broken-down window. It's raining heavily, and you know you'll have to rush home so your wife can use the car to get to her job. As you sit at your desk, are you more focused on the task at hand or your evening commute? Our children have the same kind of distractions. In urban areas, they are more often and more dramatic.

Additionally, a student with a multi-generational history of deprived needs is more likely to experience more and more intense effects from the deprived needs than a first-generation neurotic. The coping strategies are also more ingrained. The administrators, when dealing with discipline problems of second-generation neurotics are more likely to be confronted with a more intense opposition to his resolutions. There is no doubt as to why student disruptions and discipline problems in urban schools are more prevalent.

The real challenge facing our society and our schools is to determine what should be done or what is the best method of correcting the problems. How do we correct the problem of the disruptive student? Or maybe we should first agree that the bigger problem is that our whole society is experiencing the same neurotic traits. Then the question becomes, how do we correct it all? What is the best way to change what is perceived to be normal human nature?

Psychologist will agree that human behavior is a complex phenomenon. Looking through the eyes of a research scientist, one would agree that human behavior is engulfed with interacting and almost indistinguishable yet different variables. When behavioral scientists study the human phenomenon, the results are at best, erratic, and multifaceted. And the specific identifiable variables only relate to single individuals. This suggests that the Hauppauge of studied variables and the many different coping strategies (many more different variables) poised together are unsolvable. Most physical scientists do not believe that such complex problems are not solvable.

One approach used extensively by the physical scientist in solving these type problems is to lump the variables together and try to move the whole pile, looking at total results generated by the undefined, interrelated variables (interactions).

We cannot begin to study the individual variables involved with human behavior. The net thrust on our studies of human behavior should be that human behavior is learned and is therefore changeable. We must change our way of thinking; and through education, our way of thinking about how we deal with our traits, frustrations, and with one another.

To do this, we must become convinced that our human behavior is changeable—think anew, look at the facts, forget our superstitions, and be goal orientated. The basic premise on changing human behavior is simple—we can change the whole pile only through education. Our students and society must be convinced that there is good in believing that the good in each of us must be realized from within ourselves and not through the demise of others. Considering this trend of thought, we come on new and modified interpretations of the meaning and significance of self-actualization that must be ingrained into our thinking.

We should be reminded of the following parable of the shoes:

> *There was a man with no feet who was frustrated because he did not like his shoes. He did not like the way they looked, his feet hurt after walking a distance, they took too long to dry if they got wet. He was totally disgusted with the shoes until he came across a man who had no feet. He then was so elated that he had shoes and liked the feeling he derived when he compared himself with the man no feet that he begin to chop off the feet of other men so that he could enjoy more of the elation he felt when he saw other men with no feet.*

Embedded in this parable is the theory of self-actualization. True self-actualization can only be obtained from within and never through the demise of others.

Within this concept of self-actualization, greed is a good thing, and you may obtain as much wealth as you like but never through demise of others. Your accomplishments in life must be your own. Politicians must realize that they can get just as many votes through their stand on the issues and it is not necessary to demonize their competitors.

The theories of self-actualization must be taught through the internal aspects of human nature. The struggle toward self-actualization (the struggle to be all you think you can be) must be from within. The word itself may not be the best description of its meaning and perhaps should be changed to simply *internalization*. And caution is advised with this word because we must consider distorted thoughts from within.

One caution about teaching self-actualization is its relationship to morality. We must not teach self-actualization in a moralistic manner because we do not want to develop morality nor infuse a particular moral principle onto our students. But if it must be dealt with, and it does, it is far better to only interpret it rather than develop it. Morality, in the eyes of Christians as well as any number of other religions, is such an intense and emotional issue that it would take away and distort the true objectives of self-actualization and its relation to the inner self.

> "Under inner stress, a person may become alienated from his real self. He will then shift the major part of his energies to the task of molding himself, by a rigid system of inner dictates, into a being of absolute perfection. For nothing short of god like perfection can fulfill the idealized image of himself and satisfy his pride in the exalted attributes which he feels he has, could have or should have" (Horney, 1942).

In our attempts to change human behavior, we must take care to change behavior by teaching students and, hence, the public about self-actualization—the effects of it and the consequences of denial that it poses.

A good start toward a self-actualization curriculum is Karen Horney's *Neurosis and Human Growth: the Struggle toward Self Realization*. Such a program should start as soon as possible with our children and become more sophisticated and intense in teacher colleges and universities. The concept could be somewhat like teaching patriotism or the old civics classes we experienced in the 1950s, especially in the lower grades.

The benefits of such a program in our schools would be tremendous. Likewise, the effects and benefits to our public through more respect for one another, reduced crime, and a more improved harmonious society would be tremendous.

Another word of caution posed by the question, "Can white teachers teach African Americans, Latino, and other students of color a respect for one another and the benefits of self-actualization, and the consequences of not being self-actualized?" Warm and friendly teaching is not enough. The teacher must believe in the change that the target presents, understand it and its benefits, and want to reach to the target goal.

Urban schools have 7.5 million teachers; of these, 15.6 percent are people of color and 7.5 percent are African Americans. At lower grade levels, the ratios are less favorable.

It is believed that race will not be a problem in the teaching of self-actualization.

> Even with a pervasive uncertainty about others, a neurotic person may be able to give a fairly accurate description of their behavior and even of neurotic mechanism if he is trained in intelligent observation of others people.

To reach the true benefits of this concept involved with the teaching of self-actualization to teachers, the teacher colleges must first teach the teachers.

The goal of being self-actualized is to lose the neurotic obsession with our self and the neurotic effects on our inner self derived from our feelings we gain from the "other people effect"—the neurotic comparisons we make that lead us astray. With the energy gained, we become free to love and feel concern for other people and grow from within ourselves. Once we lose the neurotic obsession, we have liberated the forces leading to self-actualization—the road to unhampered growth. We must therefore teach the true meaning of the neurotic obsession.

> Logic is the humane endeavor more void of human interactions as it is born from within. It becomes more valuable when it with stands the test of human debate.

The defective characteristics of both children (students) and adults are their traits and neurotic tendencies, and they tend to intensify if not corrected. The student who defies a teacher by talking back will eventually more openly defy the teacher. And with some incidents will progress to the point of open vindictiveness and attacks similar to those exhibited by far too many adults.

Likewise, the adult or business person who commits a minor infraction will most likely repeat the offense at a more intense and serious level. Small lies eventually become large lies. Most people realize that this is a common sequence but have not made the correlation of student-to-adult infractions or to the neurotic tendencies of both. Criminal investigators have always looked at the patterns of actions to gather evidence. There appears to be a psychological accelerator within the person who strives to satisfy a neurotic need.

Again, we must make our students and, hence, the public aware of these traits (characteristics). First, that they can exist and to identify them. Eventually, we must teach them the consequences of actions related to these traits. We must teach them through education, and what better place to start the education than within our schools? We must move the whole pile of negative human traits with all their many variables toward a better understanding of one another. Understanding breeds tolerance.

The concept of our schools and the causes of their problems are entrenched deeply in the minds and beliefs of our society. They have images of bad teachers, bad and bored students, lazy and out-of-touch administrators, and multiple other reasons for our ineffective schools. The persons charged with correcting these problems mostly believe that corrections are best made through the students themselves with a system of rigid disciplines and separation between those who will and those who will not. This trend of thought is somewhat valid but is mostly not valid. But as mentioned in the previous chapters, these corrective measures and remedies for these problems have not worked, and collectively, our schools and our society have moved backward.

The remedy posed by the teaching of self-actualization challenges but only a few of the many problems facing our schools. This remedy was based on an old adage historically used to solve problems—first, identify the problem; determine its cause; then eliminate the cause. We have identified the most poignant problem (student behavior) and determined the cause (neurotic needs of students), and now we must eliminate the cause of the problems with open minds rather than with minds engulfed with neurotic thoughts and beliefs that are already embedded within many of us. We can open our minds only through education. And when our education system is defective or corrupted, we have a prelude to chaos.

Unless we can produce a better remedy for our failing schools, it is strongly advocated that we look at changing our human behavior by teaching self-actualization to the public through our schools. The following true story illustrates how pervasive the problem and traits of a neurotic public is.

While leaving a rather large drugstore, the security alarm sounded. The security personnel approached and managed to examine the startled shopper and the packages but did not verbally accuse the shopper of any thievery. The customer voluntarily removed her coat and emptied her bags and showed receipts for purchases. The real problem was that this was the third time the same incidence had happened to the same person. The store manager was questioned as to why the incidence was happening. The astonishing answer he gave was that the alarm was a deterrent to thievery. An argument ensued. The shopper argued that the deterrent was a deterrent to shopping at this particular store. The manager's argument was emphatic, and he questioned,

"How else could he prevent people from stealing?" He also stated that if the customer patronized a different drugstore, the customer would experience the same problem. He did not consider the embarrassment to the innocent customer or did not consider any other remedy such as toning down the sensitivity of the detector. His argument strongly suggested that he still believed the customer was guilty of thievery and that it was okay to cause a bit of commotion even at the expense of the innocent customer because it lets the real thieves know that the system is checking. He appeared condescending.

The points of this story are not so subtle, but consider the following: first, one of the characteristics of a neurotic person is the tendency to break down under stress, and usually the neurotic element of the augment becomes emphatic. The other point is that the store manager was young and well educated and showed some of the same tendencies that our students and many other apparently normal adults have.

Be reminded that the tenor of this book is school improvement; but we are also reminded that we, as a society, are beginning to believe that we can only negotiate through strength. Our advancement in life must be at the demise of others, that we cannot trust anyone. One must belong to the elite group to be someone and advance in life; we must bear individual arms to be protected. All other religions and governments are evil, and the list goes on with other beliefs based on neurotic concepts.

Another incident worthy of mentioning is that a local school system recently enacted a policy prohibiting students from touching one another in any form. The rationale given to national TV reporters was that touching was interfering with the learning process. Because of a zero tolerance policy, one student had been suspended for giving another a high five. This example of another policy demonstrating how we, as a society, are yielding to our neurotic tendencies—developing policies based on a rigid system of discipline.

We must attract and solve these problems.

"The remedy posed by the teaching of self-actualization challenges but only one of the problems facing our schools. It is based on old adage historically used to solve problems—first, identify the problem; determine its cause; then eliminate the cause. We must identify and determine the cause of problems with open minds rather than with a mind engulfed with neurotic thoughts and beliefs. We can open our minds only through education. And when our education system is defective or corrupted, we have a *prelude to chaos*."

CHAPTER 6

Funding Our Schools

There is no doubt that most of our urban schools are dilapidated, in a state of physical and structural decline, or lacking in space and proper teaching resources (such as computer equipment and laboratories). Moreover, some of the schools have suffered cutbacks in their athletic programs, extracurricular activities, and school-sponsored events. At the root of all of these problems is money. Our urban schools simply lack the adequate funds to operate optimally.

As with any public funding issue, there are three basic ways of resolving the problem: to raise taxes (revenue), to lower the tax rate but expand the tax base, or to optimize the way the tax revenue is obtained and used. Before discussing the options further, let's examine the process of how school funding is obtained and what factors affect the funding.

Obviously, schools receive federal money. Right or wrong, municipalities have only a marginal voice in the federal budget process. Therefore, for the purposes of this discussion, the revenue from the federal government will be considered fairly constant. Although the income stream might change over a period and with various administrations, the changes are slow; and in general, municipalities have adequate time to react to any increases or decreases in funding (excluding funding at the college level).

On the local level, municipal bonds are the primary source of funding. These municipal bonds are sold to investors in increments of $1,000-$100,000. Unlike U.S. Treasury Security treasuries (e.g. treasury bonds), the interest from municipal bonds is exempt from federal taxes. And in many cases, the interest is also exempt from state and local tax. The tax-free yield makes the investments very attractive to investors.

With regard to the states or other local entities that issue the bonds (city or municipality), the tax-exempt nature of these bonds allows the issuing entity to offer the bonds at a lower interest rate than the interest rate offered by the U.S. government. Keep in mind that the lower yield (interest payment) is still attractive to investors because of the tax-exempt nature of the investment. Therein lies the savings for the state and local municipalities.

There is also another major source of income that provides our schools with operating revenue: property tax (ad valorem tax). Simply stated, property values are assessed by the municipalities and taxed at a predetermined rate (measured in mills—$1 of tax revenue for every $1,000 in assessed property value). Taken at face value, there would not seem to be a problem-raising revenue for the schools. Municipal bonds are attractive investments, and the property taxes boost the tax base.

Unfortunately, things are not as simple as they appear because not all municipal bond were created equal, and not all property values are the same. There are several issues that affect the sale of municipal bonds. The first issue is the past bond performance of the municipality. If a city oversold bonds in the past, defaulted on bonds, or had to refinance their bonds because of financial hardship, investor confidence is shaken; and it is harder for them to sell bonds in the future. This concept is similar to someone having bad credit and applying for a loan. At best, the yield (interest rate) will be higher. It should be noted that for all major municipalities, bond-investment-rating agencies publish the ratings for the bonds.

A second problem that many municipalities encounter is that of overlapping demographics. Broward County lies within the state of Florida. Within Broward County lies the city of Fort Lauderdale. When all three entities issue bonds without a well-coordinated plan or revenue sharing and revenue redistribution, it is entirely possible that the less-affluent areas will be overburdened with taxes and the more-affluent areas of Broward County will have a surplus of revenue (elevated home values alone can do this).

Lastly, it is imperative that comptrollers, treasurers, and city planners examine the municipality's debt trend and their future financing. For example, in spite of the current economic hardships that the nation is enduring, areas such as Austin, Texas, are still experiencing positive economic growth. Because of this growth, Austin will still be able to issue bonds at their present rate (assuming their actions are currently sound). Conversely, Detroit is experiencing a severe decline in home values, high unemployment, and increasing economic uncertainty. Because of the situation in Detroit, it would be unwise to increase the revenue derived from bonds or to increase property taxes unless the money provides a direct and short-term economic benefit to the city. Stated another way, building a new football stadium might not be a good idea. Offering major corporations a one-year exemption on property tax if they move to Detroit might be a good idea because the employees who move with the company would bring in additional property tax and sales tax revenue.

As this directly pertains to our schools, it is possible to boost revenue for inner city schools without raising taxes or significantly affecting other municipalities. Perhaps the first step is to address the issue of overlapping demographics. Getting back to the example of Fort Lauderdale, Florida (this city is typical of many cities across the United States), within the Greater Fort Lauderdale area, there are the following cities and townships: Davie, Lauderhill, Lauderdale-by-the-Sea, Pompano Beach, Deerfield Beach, Lighthouse Point, and Sunrise. By having all these townships—especially in light of the property taxes (ad velorem)—the affluent children reap the benefits and the impoverished ones suffer by attending the substandard schools.

Another benefit to consolidating townships is the elimination of duplicate buildings, jobs, and jurisdictional red tape. Fewer police departments, fewer school superintendents, fewer city planners, fewer zoning laws, fewer mayors and city officials . . . and the list goes on. An even more subtle benefit is the reduction in unfunded pension liabilities. These greatly hurt the bond rating and increase the yield the municipality has to pay to the investor. And even though some money will flow out of the affluent areas into the less-affluent areas, it is indicated that the administrative savings will offset any negative benefits.

Another measure than can be taken would be to hire an investment banking firm to examine the debt structure of the municipalities. It is only prudent to confirm that the prudent and future debt structure, tax base, and revenue estimates are in line with good economic principals. Along these lines, a major change in legislation is needed in many states. At the present time, voters are allowed to decide on general obligation bond issues (bonds that are paid off using tax receipts). Although voters are well aware of whether they want a new stadium, very few voters are well versed enough in finances to know whether it makes good financial sense to use a bond and tax money to pay for such a project.

Lastly, ensure there is adequate oversight. This can be done by issuing bank-qualified municipal bonds. This type of investment tool is almost identical to the municipal bond except that it is sold to banks rather than individuals. When the bank purchases the security, the bank receives a discount. The benefit to this type of investment is that banks are encouraged in invest in municipal securities, and they take an interest in the financial well-being of that municipality. Another set of trained, watchful eyes never hurts!

Finally, and most importantly, we will move a step closer to reaching our goal of providing an equal educational opportunity to all our children.

CHAPTER 7

The Teaching of Self-actualization

The teaching of self-actualization starts with several cautions: first that of its proximity to and relation with the morality aspects of self-actualization, and second, the ethnic concerns of teaching it. It should also be known that the teaching of self-actualization in a public domain, at least as defined in this book, has not been advocated before. As such, the adaption of such a program is likely to be met with trepidation. Only guidelines for teaching are presented.

> The goal of being self-actualized is to become all that you want to be, think you can be, and feel you should be. To be self-actualized, we must lose the neurotic obsession with ourselves and the neurotic effects on our inner self derived from our feelings we gain from the "other people effect"—the neurotic comparisons we make that lead us astray. With the energy gained, we become free to love and feel concern for other people and grow from within ourselves. Once we lose the neurotic obsessions, we have liberated the forces leading to self-actualization—the road to unhampered growth. We must, therefore, teach the true meaning of the neurotic obsessions and their effect on our lives.

The goal of teaching self-actualization is to teach students to become all that they want to be, think they can be and feel they should be. And to teach students the importance of understanding their self and their inner most feelings. To become self actualized we must first lose the neurotic obsession with our selves and the neurotic effects on our inner self derived from the feeling we gain from the "Other People Affect"—the neurotic comparisons we make that lead us astray with frustrations. When self actualized, within ourselves we are free to love and feel concern for other people and grow from within ourselves with unhampered growth. We must therefore teach the true meaning of the neurotic obsessions and the effect on our lives.

Chapter 5 cautioned about the relationship of morality to self-actualization and advised that if morality must be dealt with, it would be far better to only interpret it rather than develop it. It is and was further advised that Christianity as well as any number of other religions are such an intense and emotional subject that it might take away from and distort the true objectives of self-actualization and its relation to the inner self and other concepts. Unfortunately, in the eyes of far too many religions, including Christianity, any other religion is evil. Yet all have, as one of their main concepts, issues of morality and issues involving the inner self. Therefore, in teaching the concepts of self-actualization, we must start with the idea that self-actualization is born from within each individual. As such, you do not have a claim to anything, except that which is dictated by law including gifts and that which is generated by you and your rational self—that which you learn or earn.

Any curriculum for self-actualization is best started in the lower grades, teaching the relationship of one person to another and expounding the benefits and meaning of self-respect and respect for one another. The consequences and benefits of a positive relationship between people must be emphasized alone with the inner self-aspect of relationships. The giving from within rather than receiving from outside of one's self should be emphasized. The complexity of these concepts should progress with the age (grade level) of the student and always to be emphasized one's responsibility to and for himself.

Though much more complex, the details and pedagogy should be developed by the teacher colleges using techniques similar to those used in teaching patriotism or civics. The curriculum should continue with increased intensity and awareness of self-actualization through high school and college.

Classes in the concepts of self-actualization should also be mandatory for all immigrants, mostly because the concepts of self, competition, and the role of government are so different between countries and because the number of immigrants is rapidly increasing. It must be emphasized that respect for this country does not mean disrespect for the native land just as respect for one's native country is not void of respect for this country and the relationship of respect for self and respect for others. The influx of immigrants is rapidly increasing and already has a significant effect on our school system.

The teaching of self-actualization to immigrants becomes much more important when it is realized that it is much more difficult for most immigrants to become self-actualized than born citizens—just as it is more difficult for urban students to adjust versus suburban students. It should also be noted that school administrators are beginning to note increased discipline problems with immigrant students, not realizing that the cause can be related to a lack of self-actualization.

The following represent the characteristics of good and responsible citizens:

- Are informed and thoughtful about the principles and practices of *democracy*
- Participate in their communities through membership in voluntary civil associations
- Act politically to accomplish public purposes
- Have moral and civic virtues such as *responsibility of the common good*

The above characteristics taken from the objectives of a civics class could fit well into a self-actualization class.

One of the most difficult concepts involving self-actualization from within is the concept of love. It is used here to demonstrate the complexity of teaching self-actualization. It is extremely difficult to give love and not expect love in return. However, most people will realize most problems with love are related to your love not being returned. Your need to be loved is not being met. Some students will ask, "What good is love if you do not get love in return?" Others will rationalize that if you don't love someone, who cares that I don't get their love in return. Or what happens if someone loves me, but I do not love them? Such questions are best answered through the psychology of human relations as compassion is not normally a part of self-realization. This type of question emphasizes the importance of teacher training in these areas. In this case, it would be good to explain to the student the consequences of not understanding the inner self and the possibilities of conflict within the inner self.

Any curriculum for self-actualization is most effective when started in the lower grades but can be injected at any grade. Because of the proximity of self-actualization to ethics and religion, there may be strong interactions from students depending on their background and life experiences at grade level. Teaching the relationship of one person to another and expounding the benefits and meaning of self-respect and respect for one another is extremely important at the lower grades. The consequences and benefits of a positive relationship between people must be emphasized more at the upper-grade levels alone with the inner self aspects of relationships—the giving from within rather than receiving from outside of one's self should be emphasized. The complexity of these concepts should progress with the age (grade level) of the student and always emphasizing ones responsibility to and for himself.

There is a natural tendency, and in fact in some school systems it is mandatory that teachers get into the heads of (learn about) their students. This practice is considered impractical if not impossible. Most high school teachers are responsible for about 180 students, and it is not likely that the teacher will gain an in-depth knowledge of each student. Attempts at such often leads to a perception of favoritism. The concept and implications of the "teacher's pet" is alive and well in our schools. Consider the following example:

A teacher was getting to know and like a student considered to be a good levelheaded urban student. They would hold lengthy one-on-one conversation at least once per week. One day, the conversation turned to the teacher's combat experience in the army. The teacher was asked if he had ever killed someone, and the teacher replied yes; he thought he had. The student became excited and passionately asked if he had ever gotten a "head shot." The then excited teacher asked if it really mattered. The student asked again with double passion, "Did you ever shot anyone in the head?"

The teacher's inclination was that the student was some sort of morbid crackpot and changed his impression of his favorite student. Later, and with further investigation, he concluded that the student felt locked in the ghetto, and his only way out was through the military. He really liked the army but had a morbid fear of combat. This conclusion to this day bothers the teacher after he realized that the student may have recently watched a horrible television show about combat before he started the conversation. His thoughts progressed from John McCain who was the son of an admiral's son—a third-generation military man and how he felt about combat. Would his neurotic thoughts of combat be different? Or what motivated Hillary Clinton to concoct the story about sniper fire?

The point of this story is simply that if a teacher has 180 students, he has 180 different stories, each with sometimes multiple rationales; and in most cases, the student cannot or will not fully express his true thoughts or feelings. And sometimes the same thought and life experience will move the student in different directions. If we are to change human behavior by teaching the principles of self-actualization, it cannot be done by getting into the heads of students because the variables are too many, and the interactions are too complex. We must teach to the principles, and hopefully, the pile of characteristics and thoughts that constitute human behavior will move in the desired direction.

A superficial knowledge of a student is not enough to help a student with deep-seated neurosis. Although no one could argue against a teacher's attempts to get to know as much as possible about students, but care is advised when the prime objective is to teach about the inner self. Teachers must be fully aware of the effects of their own neurosis. And teacher colleges must do a better job of preparing teachers to teach self-actualization with a better curriculum in basic psychology.

The benefits of so-called advisory practiced at many high schools and are designed so that teachers have an opportunity to get to know students is a good thing and very beneficial to students and teachers. But there is considerable discrepancy on how it is practiced in elite private schools versus urban schools. In the elite schools, it gives students genuine help with whatever is needed—help with academics or with personal issues, and it provides the student an opportunity to express themselves.

At urban schools, there is a tendency for teachers to try to get into the heads of the students because that is where they feel help is needed the most, and the students tend not to openly express their inner thoughts. The teachers tend to feel that the poor academic performance is due to poor academic discipline or poor home conditions. They do not understand why students will camouflage their true self and feelings and not willing to openly discuss their inner feelings openly. When they feel the poor academic performance is due to genetic or mental defects, they try to identify the defect and prove their presumptions. Their attempts at analyzing student's thoughts are not effective.

In teaching self-actualization, the teacher must also teach the student to be open and true to their inner self and the consequences of their inner self, divorcing themselves from the neurotic relation and thoughts of how others might relate to them. And to realize that the love and respect they receive from others is born from the love and respect that is from within their self. They must also divorce their inner self from the neurotic motives, thoughts, desires, jealousies, fears, or any other relations born from with an obsession with others.

AVOID CHAOS! AVOID THE NEUROTIC OBSESSIONS, TEACH SELF-ACTUALIZATION

Epilogue by John V. Patrick

Civilization is a descriptive term for a relatively complex agricultural and urban culture. Civilizations can be distinguished from other cultures by their high level of social complexity and organization, and by their diverse economic and cultural activities.

I am not sure how this concept of civilization began but it definitely connotes that comparisons must be made and progress is relative to our interpretations of these comparisons. Unfortunately, we have developed a culture where comparisons based on the demise and demonization of others is the norm. In doing so, we are drifting towards chaos. We have learned and are beginning to believe, more and more that this demise is a natural way of life. We have taught ourselves to band together in groups for strength to facilitate the demise and demonization. WE HAVE EVEN GIVEN IT A NAME—HUMAN NATURE.

We must reverse this trend. We must unlearn the belief that we are better because we have made others weaker and learn to grow ourselves. We, as a people, must rid ourselves of this neurotic obsession.

Thru education, we must teach ourselves that we can only be better when we gain the love and respect of others. And, we must teach ourselves how to love and respect others. In doing so , we make the inherent comparisons more meaningful.

To convince our society of the need to change our so called human nature is a formable task, simple because in measuring our progress based on the demise of others, simple mathematics and logic tells us that in the game of winning and losing, half will win and half will lose and the chaotic fight will start over and over.

Having said all this, we come to our prime objective of improving our schools. Improved discipline has to be the starting point. Our teachers will then be free to teach and our administrators will be free to administer.

Discipline issues are suspisciously missing from far too many recent publications written on school improvement issues. When teachers complain of discipline problems, they are often fired. When discipline issuers are mentioned in relation to the elite private schools (schools for hire) the school experiences the kiss of death simply because no one will pay to attend a school with discipline problems.

APPENDIX 1

Theory of Neurotic Needs
(condensed from the Internet)

While debatable, many agree that Horney's theory of neurosis is the best that exists today. She looked at neurosis in a different light, saying that it was much more continuous with normal life than other theorists believed. Furthermore, she saw neurosis as an attempt to make life bearable, as an interpersonal controlling and coping technique.

Horney thought it a mistake to think that a neurosis in adults is caused by abuse or neglect in one's childhood. She, instead, named parental indifference the true culprit behind neurosis. The key to understanding this phenomenon is the child's perception, rather than the parent's intentions, she said. A child may feel a lack of warmth and affection if a parent, who is otherwise occupied or neurotic themselves, makes fun of their child's thinking or neglects to fulfill promises, for example.

Using her clinical experience, Horney named ten particular patterns of neurotic needs. They are based on things that all humans need, but that are distorted in some because of difficulties within their lives. As she investigated them further, she found that she could clump the ten into three broad coping strategies.

The first strategy is compliance, also known as the moving-toward strategy or the self-effacing solution. Most children facing parental indifference use this strategy. They often have a fear of helplessness and abandonment, or what Horney referred to as basic anxiety. This strategy includes the first three needs: the need for affection and approval, which is the indiscriminate need to both please others and be liked by them; the neurotic need for a partner, for someone else to take over one's life, encompassing the idea that love will solve all of one's problems; and the neurotic need to restrict one's life into narrow boarders, including being undemanding, satisfied with little, inconspicuous.

Horney's second broad coping strategy is aggression, also called the moving-against and the expansive solution. Here, children's first reaction to parental indifference is anger, or basic hostility. Needs four through eight (of Horney' 10 patterns of neurotic needs) fall under this category. The fourth need is for power, for control over others, and for a facade of omnipotence. Fifth is the neurotic need to exploit others and to get the better of them. Another need is for social recognition and prestige, with the need for personal admiration falling along the same lines. The eighth neurotic need is for personal achievement.

The final coping strategy is withdrawal, often labeled the moving-away-from or resigning solution. When neither aggression nor compliance eliminates the parental indifference, Horney recognized that children attempt to solve the problem by becoming self-sufficient. This includes the neurotic needs for self sufficiency and independence and those for perfection and unassailability.

While it is human for everyone to have these needs to some extent, the neurotic's need is much more intense, Horney explained. He or she will experience great anxiety if the need is not met or if it appears that the need will not be met in the future. The neurotic, therefore, makes the need too central to their existence. Horney's ideas of neurotic needs mirrored those of Adler in many ways. Together, Adler and Horney make up an unofficial school of psychiatry and they are often referred to as neo-Freudians or Social Psychologists.

ANNEX 2

A Day in the Life of a School Administrator

PROVIDENCE, R.I.: A city school administrator was placed on leave for throwing a Dominican flag to the floor and stepping on it during an impromptu student celebration of Dominican Independence Day last week.

Robert Perkins, a vice principal, acknowledged Wednesday that he grabbed the flag from two students in a Roger Williams Middle School hallway and threw it on the floor. He also acknowledged stepping on the flag, but said he did it only because he was under stress from unrelated school problems.

"It had nothing to do with the Dominican kids, nothing to do with me being angry because of the flag," Perkins told The Associated Press. "It could have been a U.S. flag in my hands. It could have been a wad of paper in my hands. I had had it. I had been up to my neck that day. I was stressed out to the max. It could have been a baby in my hand."

Perkins, who described himself as the school's "major disciplinarian," said he was overwhelmed all day Friday because he had been dealing with teacher complaints about student behavior and absences. He encountered the celebration in a hallway during school hours, took the flag from two students and later threw it to the floor in what Perkins called a fit of "rage" unrelated to the celebration.

"I believe I stepped on the flag," Perkins said

Ysaura Paulino said her 14-year-old son told her that Perkins said the only flag he wanted to see in the school was the American flag. Perkins denied saying that.

The Providence Public School District would not release details of what happened. But Superintendent Thomas Brady said Perkins showed a lack of judgment and cultural sensitivity and had been placed on paid leave after district officials reviewed a videotape.

Perkins was asked to leave the school on Tuesday.

State Rep. Grace Diaz, who is from the Dominican Republic, said the schools need to be "more sensitive to cultural and ethnic populations they serve."

Perkins said he would accept whatever punishment he receives, but that he appreciates the school's diversity and cares about "the people I serve inside of that building."

APPENDIX 3

Vice principal: At 'wit's end'; stepped on Dominican flag

PROVIDENCE—School vice Principal said he was at his "wits' end" Friday when he threw a Dominican flag he had confiscated earlier to the floor and stepped on it.

Speaking on WPRO radio Thursday afternoon, the VP, an educator for about 30 years who was suspended with pay after the incident, gave his version of that day.

He said three students had the flag and were parading it up and down the school's hallway, which caused a "reaction" by others in the student body. He took the flag from the students because he didn't want anything to "disturb the learning" at the school.

When asked how he took the flag from the students, he said with a "moderate amount of sternness."

Said the VP, "Nothing else happened."

He said he then continued with his day. He met with a parent and teacher, checked to see how messy the cafeteria was after breakfast, dealt with kids who were inappropriately dressed and listened to another concerned teacher.

Yet he also said Friday—like the day before—"was crazy."

"At that point, I was at my wits' end. I had had it, everything was laying on me that day. I threw that flag down to the ground and I stepped . . . but I didn't do it out of anger. I did not do it out of anger with the flag, with the kids . . ."

Later, he added, "It could have been anything in my hand."

He said a food fight that happened later Friday was unrelated to the flag incident. He also denied *a report from Rep.* that he had told students he would "mop the floor" with the flag.

Asked by talk show host Dan Yorke if he ever said such a thing, he said, "Never, never, never, never."

APPENDIX 4

The following comments are worth consideration in the matter of how teachers feel about teacher education.

What Teachers Have to Say About Teacher Education

The complaints of teachers in this 1996 survey focus on the same facets of teacher-training that were reflected in "Different Drummers," a 1997 Public Agenda survey of teacher-education professors. "The greatest weakness of the courses offered in teacher education programs, according to survey responses, is that they are so enamored of theory they are of no practical use."

http://www.psychologicalscience.org/journals/pspi/pdf/pspi2_1.pdf

"Overall, the weight of the evidence tilts strongly toward a conclusion that reducing class size, by itself, does not typically affect the instructional activities that occur in classrooms." Teacher behavior changes are far more important. [Ehrenberg, R.G., Brewer, D.J., Gamoran, A., & Wilms, J.D. (2001). Class size and student achievement. *Psychological Science in the Public Interest, 2*(1).]

Evidence from Project STAR

Article by Project Star's principal investigator concludes that across-the-board class size reductions are an expensive way to make modest improvements in school outcomes.

NBPTS Teacher Certification

http://www.caldercenter.org/PDF/1001060_NBPTS_Certified.pdf [released March 2007]

An NBPTS-sponsored study of learning outcomes for all Florida teachers over a 4 year span. Found limited evidence favoring NBPTS-certified teachers but concludes that the "efficacy of NBPTS as a tool to improve student learning appears questionable." [Harris, D. N. & Sass, T. R. (2007, January 25). *The effects of NBPTS-certified teachers on student achievement.* Working Paper No. 4, Urban Institute, Center for the Analysis of Longitudinal Data in Educational Research

APPENDIX 5

What Is Special About Special Education?

Special education is governed by federal law in most educational jurisdictions. Under *Individuals with Disabilities Education Act* (IDEA), Special Education is defined as:

> "Specially designed instruction, at no cost to parents, to meet the unique needs of a child with a *disability.*"

Special education is in place to provide additional services, support, programs, specialized placements or environments to ensure that all students' educational needs are provided for. Special education is provided to qualifying students at no cost to the parents. There are many students who have special learning needs and these needs are addressed through special education. The range of special education support will vary based on need and educational jurisdictions. Each country, state or educational jurisdiction will have different policies, rules, regulations and legislation that governs what special education is. In the United States, the governing law is:

Individuals with Disabilities Education Act (IDEA)

Typically, the types of exceptionalities/disabilities will be clearly identified in the jurisdiction's law surrounding special education. Students qualifying for special education support have needs that will often require support that goes beyond what is normally offered or received in the regular school/classroom setting.

The 13 categories under IDEA include:

- *Autism*
- *Deaf or Blindness*
- *Developmental Delays*
- *Emotional Disturbance*
- *Hearing Impairments*
- *Mental Retardation*
- *Multiple Disabilities*
- *Orthopedic Impairments*
- *Other Health Impairments*
- *Specific Learning Disabilities*
- *Speech and Language Impairments*
- *Traumatic Brain Injury*
- Visual Impairments.

APPENDIX 6

COMMUNITY RELATIONS RESTRUCTURING AND SITE-BASED MANAGEMENT

The Process for Becoming a Restructured Site-Based Managed School

All Minneapolis public schools are expected to restructure and become site-based managed schools by the conclusion of the 1993-94 school year.

All schools, whether designated as restructured and site managed or not, will be held accountable for meeting Board standards for all Building Profile outcomes.

A school ready to assume the responsibilities of site-based management should submit to the Superintendent a written request. The request should include a governance plan describing:

- The process of selecting members to its leadership team or governance group, including an explanation of how prospective members indicate their commitment to active participation and meeting the needs of all groups of students enrolled in the school.
- A comparison of the make-up of the team with the racial/ethnic and socioeconomic diversity of the student body of the school.
- The numbers of students, parents, teachers, staff, community and business represented on the team. During the first year as a site-based management school, at least 25% of the membership is expected to be non-staff. By the end of the second year, non-staff participation is expected to be at least 50%.

Staff members of a school who are also parents of students at the site may serve as staff representatives to the leadership team.

- How long members serve on the team.
- How members solicit ideas from their constituencies, and how team decisions are communicated back to the constituencies.
- How the school will ensure that the rights of individuals are respected and due process is followed.
- Evidence of substantial parent, staff, and student support for the request to be designated a site-based management school.

Upon receipt and approval of this plan, the Superintendent will recommend schools for designation as site-based management schools.

Regulation MINNEAPOLIS PUBLIC SCHOOLS adopted: 2/25/92 Minneapolis, Minnesota

APPENDIX 7

2008 Graduation Rates for Rhode Island High Schools

School ▾	Municipality	Type	Pct Graduated in 4 yrs	Pct Dropped Out by end of 4th year	Pct Completed GED within 4 yrs.	Pct Still in School after 4 yrs.	Pct Graduated in 4 yrs. (2007)	Pct Graduated in 5 yrs. (2008)	5-year graduation rate
Academy of Service	Providence	Urban	0.0%	78.6%	14.3%	7.1%	10.0%	20.0%	30.0%
Alvarez HS (Adelaide)	Providence	Urban	0.0%	62.1%	0.0%	37.9%	NA	NA	NA
BEACON Charter School	Charter	Other	60.0%	32.0%	6.0%	2.0%	57.7%	0.0%	57.7%
Barrington High School	Barrington	Suburban	95.7%	2.1%	1.7%	0.4%	95.2%	0.3%	95.5%
Blackstone Academy	Charter	Other	67.9%	7.1%	3.6%	21.4%	48.7%	11.5%	60.3%
Block Island School	New Shoreham	Suburban	100.0%	0.0%	0.0%	0.0%	*	*	*
Burrillville High School	Burrillville	Suburban	76.4%	12.4%	4.0%	7.1%	71.3%	2.2%	73.5%
Central Falls Senior HS	Central Falls	Urban	52.2%	30.0%	2.4%	15.5%	50.9%	4.2%	55.1%
Central High School	Providence	Urban	62.9%	29.4%	1.4%	6.4%	60.2%	2.8%	63.1%
Chariho Regional High School	Chariho	Suburban	86.0%	9.4%	0.7%	4.0%	80.9%	0.8%	81.7%
Classical High School	Providence	Urban	93.8%	4.0%	1.1%	1.1%	95.6%	1.1%	96.7%
Cooley/ Health & Sci Tech	Providence	Urban	69.9%	24.4%	0.0%	5.8%	70.2%	6.0%	76.2%

School ▼	Municipality	Type	Pct Graduated in 4 yrs	Pct Dropped Out by end of 4th year	Pct Completed GED within 4 yrs.	Pct Still in School after 4 yrs.	Pct Graduated in 4 yrs. (2007)	Pct Graduated in 5 yrs. (2008)	5-year graduation rate
Coventry High School	Coventry	Suburban	82.8%	11.4%	2.2%	3.7%	80.6%	0.0%	80.6%
Cranston High School East	Cranston	Urban Ring	83.4%	5.1%	8.3%	3.1%	76.4%	1.7%	78.1%
Cranston High School West	Cranston	Urban Ring	88.9%	7.3%	0.7%	3.2%	88.9%	0.8%	89.7%
Cumberland High School	Cumberland	Suburban	81.6%	9.3%	1.6%	7.5%	81.1%	0.0%	81.1%
DCYF Alternative Ed	State-Operated	Other	3.8%	56.6%	24.7%	14.8%	13.0%	3.0%	16.0%
Davies Career-Tech	State-Operated	Other	67.6%	14.6%	3.2%	14.6%	72.4%	4.5%	76.9%
E-Cubed Academy	Providence	Urban	60.0%	29.5%	2.9%	7.6%	57.3%	7.8%	65.0%
E. Greenwich High School	E. Greenwich	Suburban	94.4%	1.5%	1.5%	2.6%	94.5%	0.0%	94.5%
E. Providence High School	E. Providence	Urban Ring	76.8%	17.5%	1.1%	4.5%	69.0%	3.7%	72.7%
Exeter-W. Greenwich HS	Ex-W. Greenwich	Suburban	87.6%	5.2%	2.6%	4.7%	87.1%	0.5%	87.6%
Feinstein High School	Providence	Urban	56.2%	26.7%	3.8%	13.3%	56.6%	13.2%	69.8%
Hope Arts School	Providence	Urban	50.8%	38.1%	4.0%	7.1%	55.6%	6.0%	61.7%
Hope Info Tech School	Providence	Urban	48.6%	39.2%	2.7%	9.5%	54.2%	2.1%	56.3%
Hope Leadership School	Providence	Urban	53.4%	32.3%	2.3%	12.0%	54.5%	3.8%	58.3%
Johnston Senior High School	Johnston	Urban Ring	78.6%	6.3%	8.7%	6.3%	61.8%	2.9%	64.6%
Lincoln Senior High School	Lincoln	Suburban	83.7%	12.1%	2.3%	2.0%	86.1%	1.4%	87.5%
Middletown High School	Middletown	Suburban	84.2%	5.9%	3.9%	5.9%	81.3%	1.5%	82.8%
Mount Pleasant High School	Providence	Urban	65.0%	22.6%	1.7%	10.8%	56.7%	3.8%	60.5%
Mt. Hope High School	Bristol Warren	Suburban	80.5%	10.4%	2.0%	7.2%	74.8%	4.2%	79.0%

School ▾	Municipality	Type	Pct Graduated in 4 yrs	Pct Dropped Out by end of 4th year	Pct Completed GED within 4 yrs.	Pct Still in School after 4 yrs.	Pct Graduated in 4 yrs. (2007)	Pct Graduated in 5 yrs. (2008)	5-year graduation rate
N. Kingstown Senior HS	N. Kingstown	Suburban	89.3%	5.9%	2.1%	2.7%	91.4%	0.0%	91.4%
N. Providence HS	N. Providence	Urban Ring	88.8%	4.6%	1.1%	5.6%	87.6%	1.2%	88.8%
N. Smithfield High School	N. Smithfield	Suburban	89.5%	1.6%	6.5%	2.4%	87.2%	2.3%	89.5%
NE Laborers' Career Academy	Cranston	Urban Ring	56.3%	19.4%	5.8%	18.4%	77.4%	3.2%	80.6%
Narragansett High School	Narragansett	Suburban	95.6%	2.7%	0.9%	0.9%	88.7%	1.4%	90.1%
Pilgrim High School	Warwick	Urban Ring	71.3%	13.6%	4.4%	10.7%	64.5%	1.9%	66.4%
Ponaganset High School	Foster-Glocester	Suburban	87.0%	7.7%	2.7%	2.7%	93.8%	1.4%	95.2%
Portsmouth High School	Portsmouth	Suburban	86.6%	4.6%	6.0%	2.8%	87.9%	1.4%	89.3%
Prov Acad of Int'l Studies	Providence	Urban	72.7%	21.7%	2.8%	2.8%	67.4%	1.6%	69.0%
R.I. School for the Deaf	State-Operated	Other	*	*	*	*	*	*	*
R.Y.S.E.	Chariho	Suburban	36.4%	36.4%	18.2%	9.1%	47.1%	11.8%	58.8%
Rogers High School	Newport	Urban Ring	66.7%	21.5%	3.2%	8.6%	62.1%	3.1%	65.2%
S. Kingstown High School	S. Kingstown	Suburban	87.7%	7.3%	2.0%	3.0%	85.2%	1.9%	87.0%
Scituate High School	Scituate	Suburban	84.1%	8.5%	3.7%	3.7%	85.1%	2.0%	87.2%
Shea Senior High School	Pawtucket	Urban	57.0%	26.6%	1.9%	14.6%	50.4%	3.6%	54.0%
Smithfield Senior High School	Smithfield	Suburban	88.7%	5.6%	1.4%	4.2%	85.9%	0.0%	85.9%
Textron	Providence	Urban	100.0%	0.0%	0.0%	0.0%	93.3%	0.0%	93.3%
The Met	State-Operated	Other	74.1%	12.7%	2.0%	11.2%	82.1%	8.5%	90.5%
Times2 Academy	Providence	Urban	100.0%	0.0%	0.0%	0.0%	100.0%	0.0%	100.0%
Tiverton High School	Tiverton	Suburban	82.8%	9.1%	5.1%	3.0%	80.4%	1.5%	81.9%
Toll Gate High School	Warwick	Urban Ring	77.2%	12.9%	3.0%	6.9%	68.8%	0.9%	69.7%

78 John V. Patrick

School ▾	Municipality	Type	Pct Graduated in 4 yrs	Pct Dropped Out by end of 4th year	Pct Completed GED within 4 yrs.	Pct Still in School after 4 yrs.	Pct Graduated in 4 yrs. (2007)	Pct Graduated in 5 yrs. (2008)	5-year graduation rate
Tolman Senior High School	Pawtucket	Urban	58.2%	24.3%	9.0%	8.5%	46.2%	2.1%	48.3%
W. Warwick Senior HS	W. Warwick	Urban Ring	68.4%	19.0%	3.7%	8.8%	66.6%	3.6%	70.1%
Warwick Veterans Memorial HS	Warwick	Urban Ring	70.4%	12.3%	4.9%	12.3%	66.7%	2.6%	69.3%
Westerly High School	Westerly	Suburban	89.2%	5.2%	1.7%	3.8%	90.5%	2.9%	93.4%
Woonsocket High School	Woonsocket	Urban	60.2%	27.6%	3.3%	8.9%	54.1%	2.5%	56.6%

Note: NA: Not computed; school did not exist. * Too few students to report rates

Source: Information Works! School Year 2007-08

projo.com / Timothy C. Barmann

APPENDIX 8

Comments on Dropout Rates

When 500 dropouts, ages 16-25, were interviewed, they gave many reasons for leaving school:

- 47% said classes were not interesting
- 43% missed too many days to catch up
- 45% entered high school poorly prepared by their earlier schooling
- 69% said they were not motivated to work hard
- 35% said they were failing
- 32% said they left to get a job
- 25% left to become parents
- 22% left to take care of a relative

Most dropouts report they would have tried harder if more was expected from them.

What do students suggest to improve the current situation?

- better teachers
- offer more alternatives
- schools should offer real-life opportunities
- more help with learning problems
- tutoring
- more councilors

- summer school
- more and better supervision
- more school-to-home communication
- more and better mentoring

INDEX

www.ingramcontent.com/pod-product-compliance
Lightning Source LLC
Chambersburg PA
CBHW021234280526
45784CB00005B/2103